HANUKCATS

HANUKCATS

AND OTHER TRADITIONAL JEWISH SONGS FOR CATS

LAURIE LOUGHLIN

Illustrations by GEMMA CORRELL

CHRONICLE BOOKS

SAN FRANCISCO

The author and publisher have made every reasonable attempt to determine
that the songs parodied in this work are in the public domain.

Library of Congress Cataloging-in-Publication Data

Loughlin, Laurie.
  Hanukcats and other traditional Jewish songs for cats / Laurie Loughlin.
     pages cm
  ISBN 978-1-4521-1542-9
1. Cats—Humor. 2. Hanukkah—Humor. 3. Jewish hymns—Humor. I. Correll,
Gemma, illustrator. II. Title.

PN6231.C23L685 2013
  636.8'0207—dc23

                              2012045219

Manufactured in China

Designed by Ryan Diaz

10 9 8 7 6 5 4 3 2

Chronicle Books LLC
680 Second Street
San Francisco, California 94107
www.chroniclebooks.com

For my mother and father, Laura and Richard Loughlin,
who always believed in miracles.

MY THANKS TO

CANTOR BERNARD GUTCHEON, for sharing
his music and advising me;

LEE FLOERSHEIMER, for her research assistance;

RYAN DIAZ for his fresh book designs;

APRIL WHITNEY for publicizing this feline fun;

my "menshen" past (TRUDY, MAX, GRETA,
PENELOPE, and SPIKE LOUISE) and present
(NED and REIKO)

CONTENTS

WE WANT SOME TUNA AND CHICKEN

"HEVENU SHALOM"
—FOR SHABBAT

We want some tuna and chicken.
We want some tuna and chicken.
We want some tuna and chicken.
We want some tuna, chicken,
Beef would be nice, too.

*(Repeat several times, increasing the tempo
each time.)*

KMART, KMART

"KEMAH, KEMAH"

Kmart, Kmart, go there, please.
Buy me shampoo that kills fleas.
Hanukkah is glee, eight presents for me.
Purr, purr, purr, purr, purr, purr, purr,
Purr, purr, purr, purr, purr, purr, purr,
Hanukkah is glee, eight presents for me.

How about a scratching board,
Foam balls dangling from a cord?
Catnip birds and mice would be very nice.
Purr, purr, purr, purr, purr, purr, purr,
Purr, purr, purr, purr, purr, purr, purr,
Hanukkah is glee, eight presents for me.

Get a collar that will fit,
One designed by Jaclyn Smith,
Cat rugs that won't snag, and the paper bag!
Purr, purr, purr, purr, purr, purr, purr,
Purr, purr, purr, purr, purr, purr, purr,
Hanukkah is glee, eight presents for me.

MATTED
FUR

"MA'OZ TSUR"

Matted fur all over me,
Smoothness now my coat lacks.
Being long-haired certainly
Has its cosmetic drawbacks.
Knots that thwart the hairbrush,
All attempts to tame my tress,
It just makes me feel so blah
'Cause I'll look bad for Hanukkah.
It just makes me feel so blah
'Cause I'll look bad for Hanukkah.

YOU HAVE
A LITTLE DREIDEL

"I HAVE A LITTLE DREIDEL"

You have a little dreidel
With which I'd like to play,
The minute you're not looking,
I'll spirit it away.

Dreidel, dreidel, dreidel,
With which I'd like to play,
Dreidel, dreidel, dreidel,
I'll spirit it away.

I have a lovely body
With legs so long and thin.
My paw will fling the dreidel
And make it spin, spin, spin.

Dreidel, dreidel, dreidel,
My legs are long and thin.
Dreidel, dreidel, dreidel,
I'll make it spin, spin, spin.

I don't care what it stops on,
Nun, gimel, he, or shin.
I make up my own rules, and
Whichever one, I win!

Dreidel, dreidel, dreidle,
Nun, gimel, he, or shin,
Dreidel, dreidel, dreidel,
Whichever one, I win!

TINY BOW

"HI 'NE BO"

Tiny bow atop your dress,
I can pull it out, I guess.
I will jump right
Upon your lap,
And that tiny bow I'll snap!
I will jump up on your lap, and
    that tiny bow I'll snap!

OH,
YARMULKES

"OY HANUKA"

Oh, yarmulkes! Oh, yarmulkes!
Our precious little caps,
We wear you to the synagogue
And also taking naps.
Cotton, wool, and satin,
Opaques and sheers,
When perched atop our heads, they
Complement our ears.

In neons and pastels,
They won't blow off even in
   a breeze.
They decorate our uppers.
We put them on for suppers
And sometimes even when we're
   climbing trees.

Oh, yarmulkes! Oh, yarmulkes!
You helped make history
When we reclaimed our holy Temple
Back in B.C.E.
After all we did, it's
So annoying that
Nobody ever mentions
The Maccabees were cats!

In neons and pastels,
We flowed like a rainbow down the hill.
We frightened Antiochus.
His legions could not knock us.
We love you, yarmulkes, and always will!

HANUKKAH MESSES

"CHANUKA BLESSINGS"

I goofed today in the den,
Lost my breakfast shortly after ten.
I left my mark upon the brand-new rug
And on presents so brightly wrapped
For Hanukkah. Uuh-oh.

I goofed at lunchtime once more,
Knocked a pan of latkes on the floor.
Hot oil spilled across linoleum
Which was warping as it flowed.
Everyone saw me, too. Uuh-oh.

I goofed this evening again,
Swiped the shammes, buried it and then
Came back inside where Uncle Clyde
Some wax he spied
On my whiskers. Uuh-oh.

LET
ME GLOAT

"L'VIVOT"

I am a star. Let me gloat, emote.
Let me gloat, emote. You can dote.
Let me gloat, emote. You can dote.

You shall attempt to please me.
You shall attempt to please me.
You shall attempt to please me,
Please me for Hanukkah.

JUST ONE NIGHT'S WORTH OF OIL

"Y'LADIM BANEYROT"

Just one night's worth of oil
Could we light for our toil,
Our Maccabee win to celebrate.
By a miracle one night turned into eight.
Our Maccabee win to celebrate,
By a miracle one night turned into eight.

We were fueled from on high.
When our feat caught His eye,
One lampful was turned into vats.
Yes, and that's how we became the
    Hanukcats!
One lampful was turned into vats.
Yes, and that's how we became the
    Hanukcats!

IT'S
NOT
ENOUGH

"DAYENU"
—FOR PASSOVER

Thank you for the
    shank bone
And the haroset and
    matzoh bread.
We do appreciate your
    good intentions, but
It's not enough.
It won't suffice.
We're still hungry.
We need more food
    this very minute!

HAVE
A BURRITO

"HAVA NAGILA"
—FOR CELEBRATIONS

Part 1 (A)   Have a burrito.
               Beef bits are neato
               Especially when you
               Drop them on the floor.
               Gefilte fish are
               Something we wish for.
               Give us a dish or
               Leave an open jar.

Part 2   We'll do the kitchen floor.
               Don't worry 'bout that chore.
               We'll clean up every crumb
               Like all good cats should.
               We love the holidays.
               It's not a passing phase.
               Big celebrations mean
               That we get more food.

               Me-ow. Meow. Meow. Meow. Meow!

Part 3   Now is the time to start the seder.
Please don't decide to make it later.
Now is the time to start the seder.
Please don't decide to make it later.
Aren't you starved?
Wouldn't you like
To sink your teeth into a feast?

Part 1 (b)   If we finagle
One from the table,
We'll start things rolling
With a matzoh ball.
We're catching glimpses
Of those cheese blintzes,
So appawtizing,
And they'll feed us all!

(Repeat parts 2 & 3)

I'VE GOT
LOVE HANDLES

"SHINE LITTLE CANDLES"

I've got love handles 'round my tum.
Hanukkah is here.
I lick my chops and dig right in
When those treats appear.
Pat my love handles, one by one,
Eating is such fun.
I'll stretch and yawn and go to sleep
When Hanukkah is done.

WHAT IS
THAT SMELL?

"MI Y'MALEL"

What is that smell
That floats from the kitchen?
What is that smell?
Whether a chop,
A rump, or a brisket,
It smells swell.

Open the door
So we can get more
Of that aroma.
What is that smell?
Oh, pray, won't you tell us
Right away.

    Aaah…
Left to our imaginations
    Aaah…
We will conjure up temptations
    Aaah…
Picturing a plate of every kind.
Won't you help restore our peace
    of mind?

(*Repeat as a round.*)

SILLY ONE

"S'VIVON"

Silly one, spin, spin, spin.
Try to catch your tail again.
Hanukkitten, you will learn
When to turn and not to turn.
I will give you everything.
To my life great joy you bring.
Circling 'round this special time,
Hearts together, yours and mine.

IN A ROW
I LIGHT YOU

"HANEYROT HALALA"

In a row, in a row,
In a row I light you.
In a row I light you,
Eight pretty candles blue.
Hanukkah will end,
But not its inner glow.
Eight candles represent
The joy we've come to know.
Let's dance the hora,
Join in a circle of paws.
Hanukcat menorah,
It's mine and yours.

LISTEN
AND
FOLLOW US

"LISTEN AND FOLLOW ME"

Listen and just follow us.
There are things we must discuss.
Hanukkah is on the way,
But have you hugged your cat today?
You get busy and forget
To take time to pet your pet.
Now, what is all this mishegoss?
We still need you to love us.

Listen and just follow us.
There are things we must discuss.
Hanukkah is on the way,
Big preparations every day.
All these special meals you do,
We demand a bite or two.
You can't expect us to stay calm.
So much food just turns us on!

I SURE
MISS HIM

"AL HANISIM"

I sure miss him.
He is my buddy.
He went to college.
My life's all bollixed.
We used to run and play,
But then he went away.
He's coming home for
    Hanukkah today!

I sure miss him.
Of all the family,
He is the one who
I'm most attached to.
Now I can hardly wait
Till he comes through
    the gate.
He's coming home for
    Hanukkah today!

IT'S ME
YOU PICKED

"MI ZE HIDLIK"

It's me you picked to be your cat.
I'm glad I'm not alone,
And finally I will get to spend
 A Hanukkah at home.
La la la la la la
 La la la la la la
La la la la la la
 Hanukkah at home.
La la la la la la
 La la la la la la
La la la la la la
 Hanukkah at home.

All cats will do their best to keep
The holy days on their own.
But it's so nice when they can spend
 A Hanukkah at home.
La la la la la la
 La la la la la la
La la la la la la
 Hanukkah at home.
La la la la la la
 La la la la la la
La la la la la la
 Hanukkah at home.

MY
MEZUZAH

"MY CANDLES"

My mezuzah is fastened to the door.
I like to chew it 'cause that is what it's for.
It's got my toothmark.
It's looking so sharp
On this the first day of Hanukkah.

My mezuzah is fastened to the door.
I like to chew it 'cause that is what it's for.
It's got two toothmarks.
It's looking so sharp
On this the second day of Hanukkah.

(*Repeat, changing the numbers to the appropriate day
of Hanukkah.*)

HANUKCATS

"HANUKAH"

Hanukcats, Hanukcats,
Honor those today.
Hanukcats, Hanukcats,
Who have led the way.
Hanukcats, Hanukcats,
Stubborn, sleek, and strong.
Hanukcats, Hanukcats,
Who were never wrong!